The Art of
Walking Upright

Tuesdays Will never b the
same but OUR memories of them
with you's will B
  Keep smiling
  Kia Kaha (B. Strong)

avohanui (lots of Love)
May Kemp
JKemp

3·7·07·

The Art of
Walking Upright

Glenn Colquhoun

STEELE ROBERTS LTD
Aotearoa New Zealand

to Barbara

3rd printing ~ 2003

Published with the assistance of the
Willi Fels Memorial Trust

Cover design Lynn Peck

Published by Roger Steele
STEELE ROBERTS LTD
Box 9321 • Wellington • Aotearoa New Zealand

Phone (04) 499 0044 ~ Fax (04) 499 0056
books@publish.net.nz ~ www.publish.net.nz

1-877228-20-6

CONTENTS

TE TII, MANGONUI

Waiata aroha   10
Love song   11
Jumping Ship   13
Tom Kelly's laundry   15
Birdsong   16
Threading the needle   17
The menu   18
Whare   20
Housie, 7.30pm, Top Marae   23
Collecting pipi   24
Lament   25
Hemi George's driveway   27
The party   28
Glossary   30
The laugh   31
The trick of standing upright here   32
A problem while translating the Treaty of Waitangi   34
Waves of settlement   35
Bred in South Auckland   36
Race relations   38
The indigenous Pakeha   40

NGA POUPOU

Aunty Riwa   45
Nana   47
Uncle Bill   49
Aunty Kare   51
Uncle Tu   53
Aunty Rongo   55
Aunty Maude   57
Aunty Huia   59
Aunty Flu   61

WHAKAPAPA

    i. the taniwha   64

   ii. the underworld   66

  iii. the tide   67

  iv. carrying baggage   68

   v. a pakeha spiritual   71

  vi. the bird   72

 vii. the half moon   75

viii. a story   76

  ix. pakeha dreaming   78

LEARNING HOW TO HONGI

  Te huihuinga ki waho   81

  Wero   82

  Karanga   83

  Haka   85

  Whakaekea   86

  Karakia   87

  Mihi   88

  Waiata   90

  Koha   91

  Hongi   92

  Whakanoa   93

  Glossary   94

My name is Glenn Colquhoun and I am Pakeha. My ancestors were from Scotland and Wales and England and Germany. Some came via Tasmania. I think that some were Jewish. Most of them came here five generations ago.

I grew up in South Auckland. I remember eating potato salad with beetroot in the middle and pineapple pie at the Cook Island church my father built. I watched the people there place mats on a couple at a wedding I went to once. I ate taro and chop suey at my brother-in-law's place. His family is Samoan. I watched his old people stand and speak at weddings and funerals and birthdays I went to. I watched them dance the Siva. I remember going home from Palagi socials with him and stopping for Kentucky Fried Chicken on the way.

My earliest contact with things Maori was being hugged by Mrs Roi at church. She was so soft. Even when she talked to me it was like being hugged. I still feel five years old when I see her. I still get squashed in her arms.

For all this I grew up firmly in a Pakeha world. I looked over the fence at things Polynesian and Maori. I recognised lots of sights and sounds and patterns but not what they meant.

These poems are poems I wrote in Te Tii, the home of Ngati Rehia of Ngapuhi in the Bay of Islands. It is a place I went to stand on the other side of this fence, a place I finally went to learn things Maori. In the end it became a year full of aunties and uncles and children and doing dishes. For these experiences and relationships I think I am the luckiest Pakeha I know. I found there old ways of being so long forgotten inside me that they felt new.

These poems then are about belonging. They are about discovering a place to stand within a Maori world. Ultimately for me they are about finding more clearly what it means to be Pakeha and what it means to be human.

Acknowledgements

My greatest thanks to Ngati Rehia for their continued love, patience and good humour towards me. E hoa ma, he mihi nui tenei ki a koutou katoa mo to koutou aroha ki ahau. Na koutou katoa ahau i atawhai. Na koutou katoa i homai nga mea pai o te ao ki ahau, to koutou koa, to koutou pouri, to koutou reo. E kore ahau e wareware ki a koutou.

The poems *Aunty Riwa, Uncle Bill,* and *Aunty Kare* have been previously published in *Printout.*

Thanks also to Diane Brown for her advice on the poetry and to Di Blanch for her help with the photography. A big thanks to Christine Roberts and Roger Steele for publishing the poems, and especially for understanding where they come from.

Arohanui, Glenn

Te Tii, Mangonui

Waiata aroha

No te ngahuru ka kitea koe e ahau
i Te Tirohanga Mutunga o Kerei Mangonui
i Tana Tuahine. E ngahoro ana nga rau.
I hikoi ahau i te huarahi kirikiri.
I korero taua i tetahi po awatea noa.
Nau ahau i whangai ki te kumara me te taro parai,
ka moe ahau. E mahana ana te ahi.
No muri ka waiata ahau i nga waiata maene,
ka kanikani koe. I te koanga ka haere ahau.
Kua tupu ano nga taru.

I te koanga ka haere ahau.
Kua tuwhera te rangi penei me te putiputi.
I haere ahau i te ara ki te wahi i noho-ai-ahau-i-mua.
E iri ana aku kakahu i roto i te kapata. I kai ahau
i nga hanawiti me te tihi. I moe ahau i te moenga ngawari.
I tetahi po, i roto i taku moe, ka rongo ahau i nga ua ra
e maringi ana i taku tuanui. Ko te marama
tou kanohi i te matapihi. Kahore ahau i hiahia ki te ara
engari kia werohia aku waewae ki nga kohatu.
I pirangi ahau kia ngahoro nga rau.

Love song

It was autumn when I found you.
At that place where Matiretoha-waved-goodbye.
The leaves were falling.
I had been walking on a stone road.
One night we talked until the morning.
You fed me sweet potato and fried bread
and then I slept. The fire was warm.
Later I sang smooth songs and you danced.
I left when it was spring.
The grass was growing back.

I left when it was spring.
The sky had opened like a flower.
I took the road that led me back to where I was before.
My clothes still hung in the wardrobe. I ate
sandwiches and cheese. I slept in a soft bed.
One night I dreamt I heard your rain falling on
my roof again. The moon was your eye in
the window. I did not want to wake at all.
I wanted stones to prick my feet.
I longed for leaves to fall.

Jumping ship

Because blue water leaves lipstick at night on the beach.

Because of the smell of seawater.

Because the taste of the sun is of watermelon.

Because of the way food is eaten.

Because life grows fat like fruit on trees.

Because I saw the night swallow the day like an oyster.

Because time is a thick slice of bread.

Because houses stir like cattle on grass.

Because quiet is prepared so noisily.

Because people stretch like cobwebs.

Because ghosts cling like mist to the hollows.

Because a drum collects water from a hole in a roof.

Because everything sticks like a word on the tip of my tongue.

I have jumped ship.

Tom Kelly's laundry

I'm sure Tom
Kelly's laundry is alive,
the way it snaps
on the line
like a guard dog,
or flickers like fish in a net.
Its arms reach out
to grab me
when I walk past
like ghosts waiting
for someone to scare.
Tea-towels play a piano
to add some spooky music.
Seagulls try
to pick a fight.
I have never seen them
dry like normal clothes.
Instead they twist on
some No 8 wire
over the last scrap of grass
before the beach
as though they were
seaweed
left at high tide struggling
or a brightly coloured
sail on a ship.
Sometimes I see
a giant mouth,
strung in mid-air, talking.
The conversation
spins around.
It keeps me laughing
in the day with its chatter
and winks back the
next morning walking
past stretched still on
someone's skin.

Birdsong

A seagull sounds like a rusty hinge on
the door of the long drop.

It is first light.

In the tree outside a sparrow chatters over breakfast.

This is the noise I make walking
in wet jandals to check the net.

For morning tea a blackbird imitates
the roll of water along the spouting.

The rain has stopped.
The mist lifts slowly off the sea.

Through the haze of the sun in the middle of the day
the wings of a shag make no noise at all.

I can hear my eyes blink.

A stilt barks like a dog in the distance.

The kahawai birds splash.
It is afternoon.

Before dusk a tui rings her bell for prayer.
The sound falls down out of her mouth, onto my roof
and against the tank of water at the front door.

It bounces on the ground.
It rests beside the cat which turns its head.

At night a morepork calls his name while I listen.
I wonder if 'morepork' is morepork for George.

At two o'clock in the morning I hear the sound
of a voice driving over a cattle grate. It comes
from the house on the hill above me.

I think that Buck has won another hand.

Aunty Maraea manages to laugh and curse at the same time.
A queue of dogs begins to bark. She calls him a bloody bugger.

I am not sure what sort of birds are these.

Threading the needle

Wii walks
every day
back and forth
across this circle.

With two arms
that look like fingers
holding a needle
he stitches
the soil
together where
it doesn't
quite meet
at the road.

He is
lacing
us up
with the scratch
of his shoes
on the stones.

A cigarette
is in his mouth
like a piece of cotton
torn off
the reel.

The menu

The kumara is subtle,
An opulent honey,
The powerful memory of woodsmoke
and the arrogance of petrol.
After the hangi Hemi wants the sacks
he has been using to collect the oil
which still drips from his car.

The corn is vintage,
One or two months at least.
It has matured in the stream
that runs at the back of the bush.
The pungent eye-watering aroma
conceals its supporting acidity.
I call it the cruel gruel.
It makes Uncle Bill fart.

The pork bones are rare.
The meat is a suggestion.
It is a tuft of hair on a bald head.
The juice dribbles down
through an old woman's beard.
This is the only joint she has ever smoked.

The kina are controversial,
The delicate ambivalence of a rich full cream
marinated in a lingering saltwater,
A mandarin from the sea.
I don't like the black bits.
The shells are good for potholes.

The oysters are alive,
Small pools of boiling mud, or in pairs
two eyes opening after a hard night.
Placed imaginatively in a row
I see the great shimmering bellies
of dancing girls.

The shellfish are a centrepiece.
They haka in the pot.
The periwinkles spin.
The crayfish stamp their feet.
Pipis poke out their tongues
And the mussels flex.
Hi ! Ha ! Hi ! Ha !

The fish heads are ferocious.
Their mouths water.
Sometimes their eyes stare around
the room and lock all the doors.
They use cabbage leaves for napkins
and rattle on their plates.
Their fins are the shape of forks.

I always say my grace.

Sometimes here you eat the food.
Sometimes the food eats you.

Whare

If I fix the step outside
it will not creak or bulge like an armful of groceries
ready to drop me.

And if I fix the window by the clock
then it will not open its mouth like a child
to taste the rain slanting from the south.
A broom sweeps the wet into a neat pile
in line with the gap at its top and the sky.

If I fix the hole cornered
in one elbow of this tin jersey
it will not rob the heat from my fire in winter,
or leave a gap of frayed wood and iron
for the cold to poke its finger on my skin.

And if I fix the gaps outside
where birds nest against the wind
they will not bang on my roof in the night
or scratch me awake in the morning.

If I cover the thin ribs above me
or the bare frame inside this belly
I will not see the fine webs tying it together.
I will not see the great heart which beats
inside this whare between its bones.

And if I paint the steady walls
they will not talk to me of
the places where they stood last,
of the pieces of building they were in another life,
of the stories in their layered colour.

And if I fix this break in my heart
let it leave a rough scar from
the rough stitches placed in me
through the slants of light in this ceiling
where nails used to cling.

And when I leave this old shell
found on an arching beach
let me always hear,
when it is pressed to my ear,
the sound of the sea.

Not wanting any more than this.
Not wanting any less.

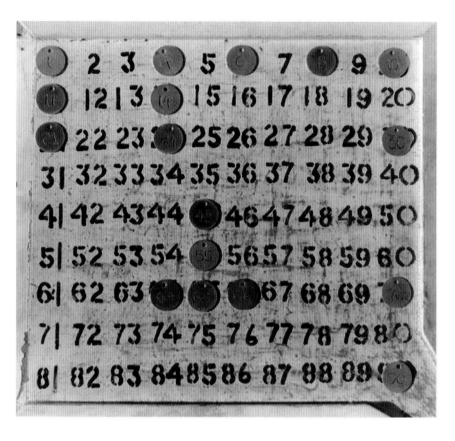

Housie
7.30pm
Top Marae

Bung in the lung number one.
Tommy Hicks number six.
Pearly gate number eight.
All the legs eleven.

Two one key to the door.
Seven O blind seventy.
Two four a couple of doz.
One four a stone.

Half way forty five.
Three O blind thirty.
Aunty Lizzy's getting dizzy.
All the sixes clickity.

All the fives fifty five.
Tom Brown is broke.
Uncle Jerry's had enough.
He's going for a smoke.

Aunty Riwa's in a fever.
Simbo is in limbo.
Uncle Buck is out of luck.
You should hear the lingo.

Barry John number ten.
Gracie's lost her place.
Some old bitch is getting rich
swears Alfred while he waits.

On the floor number four.
Aunty Rongo's betting.
Aunty Maude speaks to the Lord.
Aunty Sui's sweating.

Six four sixty four.
Next door Whiskey Bill.
Top-of-the-show bingo.
Each week this house is full.

Collecting pipi

I wrestle
in the sea's mouth
for a handful of pipi.

One balances
between my knuckles.

They leave
suckingly
and clatter
at the bottom
of the bucket.

Quietly
the sea feels
with a tongue
round the holes
in her still-hidden
gums.

She mutters under her breath
to the tide
who it seems

is always out
when you need him.

Lament

It does not matter if it is raining,
if the run-off from my roof
looks like hair blown wild against the shed,
or if the front door trembles like a lip.

Buck has gone out fishing.
The sea hides beneath his boat.

It does not matter if it is hot,
if windows poke out their tongues for a drop of water
or if trees keep their shadows tightly to themselves.

Buck has gone out fishing.
The sun swims coolly in the sea.

It does not matter if there is trouble,
if people do not speak to each other,
or if the world just seems to spin too quickly.

Buck has gone out fishing.
Seaweed anchors round his line.

It does not matter if I am happy,
if the grass is carpet on my feet,
or if the sky is a warm blanket above me.

Buck has gone out fishing. The tide rolls over
like a dog with its belly being scratched.

It does not matter if I am sad,
if my eyes are grey rocks in a stream
or if my chest is a suitcase I have to sit upon.

Buck has gone out fishing.
The salt catches in my eye.

It does not matter if he is gone,
if the forest is short one ordinary tree,
or if there is laughter missing from the night
like one more gap in a row of teeth.

Buck has gone out fishing.
Seagulls flock like angels in the distance,
waiting for a catch.

Hemi George's driveway

Hemi George's
driveway
vomits
down
the hill
and dries
in half digested
chunks of
mud.

It is
a
tongue
poking.

Driving up it
is a
prayer.

An act of faith
in first gear.

Driving down it
is cathartic

revisiting your
childhood
emptied
down a slide
and not really
knowing
how to land.

The party

Slotted in my bed
on side A
I listened while you
slowly unwound
like a tape.

I heard you say
you'd like to teach the world to sing,
that down in Jamaica they've got lots of pretty women
so I fooled around and fell in love,
I found my thrill on blueberry hill.
Wild thing you made my heart sing.
But everybody plays the fool,
And since my baby left me
I found a new place to dwell.
Welcome to the Hotel California
or the House of the Rising Sun.
Are you lonesome tonight?
I've got those lonely, lonely, lonely heartsick blues.
I'm over in the corner weeping all alone.
"Oh Maybelline — why can't you be true?"
She was a long cool woman in a black dress.
She's the devil in disguise.
She ain't nothing but a hound dog.
I can't stop loving her.
Then out in the factory
where the lights come from
the Mazda man put his thinking cap on.
He called the doctor — woke him up
said "doctor ain't there nothing I can take"
said "take a sad song and make it better"
— love potion number nine.

Well he took the words right out of my mouth.
Let's just kiss and say goodbye.
So please release me let me go,
and Hugo said you go and I said no you go,
and goodbye yellow brick road.
Gone were the dark clouds that had me bound.
I got a peaceful easy feeling,
helped me make it through the night.
Here comes the sun.
I can't stand the rain.

At four o'clock
in the morning
when it stopped
I got out of bed
and turned over
onto side B
hoping that it would
start again.
The wind plucked
the telephone wires
with its teeth.
The sea tapped
its foot on
the beach.

Glossary

Hangi, n. *Earth oven*. The old man's skin clung like sacks on a hangi. His eyes steamed. His lips were leaves of cabbage. His tongue was a shovel.

Mimi, v.i. *Make water*. At night I mimi in wet grass. My feet are cold. Starlight catches in the stream. Above me is the milky way.

Te Ua, n. *The rain*. Te Ua is a flock of birds squabbling over fish. Sometimes she is the smoke from green manuka. The kahawai dry like washing. Small embers catch on the grass.

Tio, n. *Rock-oyster*. The wheels of a car drive over the empty tio — small flowers open on the road. My neighbour farts — the sound of eating toast.

Hoha, a. *Wearisome*. 'You're a real bloody hoha — you know that — waste my time. I don't know why I bother with you buggers' said the ageing grandmother aggressively. A gumboot falls harmlessly in the distance.

Korero, n. *Talk*. That night the korero was good. It filled the room like wood-smoke. Our mouths were full, much fatter than kina. They were sweeter than the tea.

Waiata, v. *Sing*. The old women waiata. Their feet are bent claws on a branch. Their coats are made from feathers. A bird on the roof stops to listen.

Whare, n. *House, hut, shed*. This whare is an old cat. She curls up softly in the grass. Outside, a rough tail thumps. Inside, I hear the sound of breathing.

Mihi, n. *Acknowledgement, greeting*. That mihi was a round red sign on a busy road. Time stops. His fingers tap on the steering wheel. Ahead of him people walk into a meeting-house like children on a pedestrian crossing.

Whakairo, n. *Carving*. She sat quietly beside the whakairo, a mud-coloured totara — heavily lined. Her back leant up against the wall. Two feet stretched out in front. The timber got up to leave.

The laugh

for Rei

I know it's coming.

Your rubber mouth pulls back tight.

A chin disappears in your collar.

The cigarette sits like a fuse.

Your tongue strikes your lips
with a match.

I duck and wait.

Your face detonates.
The sky is a red throat.

The noise is a mushroom cloud.

Afterwards
some sound arrives.

Thunder after lightning.

My ears cling
to the side of my head.

The trick of standing upright here

Not I, some child, born in a marvellous year,
will learn the trick of standing upright here.

~ Allen Curnow
The skeleton of the great moa in the
Canterbury Museum, Christchurch

The trick of standing upright here
is the trick of using both feet.

Being born is casting on a row of stitches.
It is a whenua in a plastic bag in the freezer.

Bread is walking back from a dairy with milk.
It is the smell inside of tea-towels.

Red is the sun burning at dusk.
It is kowhaiwhai curling around a rafter.

Meeting is the grip inside a hand.
It is the sound of wet lips.

Black is the colour of the sky at night.
The clothes of old women at church.

White is the sun's paint.
Flax drying on a fence.

A feast is the warm order of plates on a tablecloth.
It is a fat kettle of tea squeezing between tables.

Seafood is a fish on the plate with lemon.
It is the rattle of cockles in a pot.

Singing is the wind in the trees like a choir.
It is Tom Kelly crooning at three in the morning.

Laughter is the sound of hands clapping.
It is a row of cans falling off a shelf.

Sleep is the feel of clean sheets on skin.
The soft gaps between people on floors.

The sky is a lid left off a tin of biscuits.
It is a man making love to a woman.

The sea is an uneven playing field.
It is the blue eyes of god.

Remembering is a statue in a park.
It is a face carved in wood.

Growing old is a pattern fading on a dress.
It is collecting pipi at low tide in an apron.

Dying is a casket the shape of a keyhole.
It is a long walk north to the cape.

The art of walking upright here
is the art of using both feet.

One is for holding on.
One is for letting go.

A problem while translating
the Treaty of Waitangi

A pakeha version:

A maori version:

THE FIRST ARTICLE

I am the boss.

THE FIRST ARTICLE

You are the boss.

THE SECOND ARTICLE

You are the boss.

THE SECOND ARTICLE

I am the boss.

THE THIRD ARTICLE

Now that's sorted out
put some clothes on,
pay your rates,
get a job
and find a lawyer.

THE THIRD ARTICLE

How about those muskets?

Waves of settlement

Sometimes settling
can be very unsettling.

To begin with there should
be a place to settle.

A settlement for this settlement
will need settling.

If the settlement
reached by this settlement
is unsettling it should be settled
so that the settlement of settlements
can be settled.

There may need to be settled
a settlement for settling any unsettling
arising from the settlement
settled for settling.

Any breaches to this settlement
will need settlement.

There could then be settlement
of the settlement and settlement
of any breaches of the settlement
for settling the settlement
of settling.

Even settlements
for settling any unsettling arising
from the settlement of breaches
to the settlement for settling settling
could be settled.

Is that settled?

Bred in South Auckland

I drive a car that is falling apart.
There is bog in the body.
There is rust in the doors.
Occasionally it does not have a warrant.
Sometimes I sleep in large rooms full of people.
I eat too much fried bread.
I am late to meetings.
I go to housie
My nose is flat.
I say Raw - tore - loo - uh.

Some people think I am a bloody maori.

I have been to university.
I have a student loan.
I photocopy my tax returns.
Most mornings I read the newspaper.
I make lists of things I have to do and like to cross them off.
I cut apples into quarters before I eat them,
Then I cut the pips out.
I put my name on things.
I listen to talkback radio.
I use EFTPOS.

Some people think I am a typical pakeha.

Last week I drove through a red light,
I did not slow down at a compulsory stop,
I changed lanes on the motorway and did not use my indicator.
When I was a boy I went to see *Enter the Dragon*,
I took one lesson in kung fu.
My parents made me do my homework.
My brother gave me chinese burns.
I like beef and pork flavoured two minute noodles.
I light incense when the house smells.
Once I dug a garden.

Some people think I am a blasted asian.

When I was a boy I learnt to swear in Samoan,
I went to school in Mangere.
I played rugby in bare feet,
Sometimes I shop at the Otara markets.
My family come from overseas.
I used to work in a factory.
Once I helped to cook an umu.
When it is summer I wear a lavalava.
I drink pineapple juice.
I like to eat corned beef.

Some people think I must be a flaming coconut.

I think I am the luckiest mongrel I know.

Race relations

My great great grandfather was from Luss.
This is a village on the shores of Loch Lomond.
My parents hang his coat of arms on their wall.

My great great grandmother was a Murray
She lived in Glasgow, by the Clyde.

I don't know if their families fought
but I wouldn't be surprised.

Some Murrays live in Whangape.
I guess we are related
except that I am Pakeha
and they are part Te Rarawa.

Somewhere along the line
I have managed to colonise myself.

It is not the first time this has happened.

My grandmother's grandfather is from England.

This has been a problem for the Scots.

I can't forget what I did to myself at Culloden.

Or what Edward Longshanks
did to William Wallace in *Braveheart*.

I still hate the bastard which of course I am.

And if that's not bad enough
my grandmother's grandmother is German.

And so is my grandmothers's mum.

One half of me has lost a war the other half has won.

Even more complicated is the fact
that my mother's father's family are Jacobs
which if I'm not mistaken makes us Jewish,

who of course won't speak to the Germans.

No-one mentions they were from Tasmania.

Sometimes I don't know how to live with myself.
I am a civil war.

The australians fight the english
        and keep the scottish happy.
The scottish fight the english
        and then they fight themselves.
The english are offended
        and won't speak to the germans.
This annoys the germans
        who of course annoy the jews.
The pakeha think they own the place.
The maori want us all to go home.

I would if I knew where that was.

Sometimes it seems I'll never win.
Sometimes I never lose.

The indigenous Pakeha

I am not the first man my wife ever loved.

I am not my parents' oldest son.

My car is second hand.

There are times when I had to wear
my older brother's shirts.

Sometimes I have worn my father's pants.

The house I live in is not new.

The curtains were my mother's.

The floor was a tree.

The windows are a shovelful of sand
from a white beach.

According to a four by two
Wiki woz hair before me.

I am not the first person to think
that the moon is a slice of cheese

or that the land is the belly
of a fish poking out of the sea.

I have read that the earth is not flat.

The stars are round.

They look jagged to me.

When I speak I speak in Greek.

I count in Babylonian.

I took god from some missionaries

who took him from Rome
who took him from Greece
who took him from the Jews.

The Jews just flogged him.

I was not the first man to arrive here.

He came from somewhere else.

I bought the land from someone
who bought the land from someone

who bought the land from someone
who probably stole it.

The sun rises in the east.

The weather comes in from the west.

I drink tea in china.

My neighbour's dog still barks at me,
I think he is Alsatian.

Either I don't belong to anyone,

Or else I'm indigenous everywhere.

NGA POUPOU

Aunty Riwa

Her face is a set of eyes in a painting that look at you no matter where you shift, so that if you hide in the sea you will find them in green water, lapping, and in the open mouths of fish, and if you hide in the sky you will see them peering roundly at dawn over the edge of the land, where clouds like fists will rub away their bloodshot, and if you run into the ground you will see them in the twinkle of quartz between dull rocks shut tight like her eyelids, you will see fine wrinkles of gold in her face, and if you close your eyes against her they will still be heard in the round sound of water splashing or of people talking or of a plate rolling softly on the top of a table, and even if you hide in the forest, or this bush of words written by the lines of her face, you will still see her watching in the eyes of birds and of spiders and of curled ponga until you feel, in a pause, at the end of a twisting sentence, that even the writing has been reading you.

Nana

She is a big slow bus
                    on a narrow road.

There is no room to pass on the right.

There is no room to pass on the left.

Children stare from a back window
like chickens under a hen's wing.

Their noses press against the glass.

A bumper collects dents.

Wrinkles initial the dust.

Her gears cough.

She is always smoking.

It does not matter what hurry you are in.

You will always have to slow down.

Uncle Bill

There is the sound of a chair under the table.

The sound of a knife on the plate.

Water pouring from a jug.

A spoon in a cup.

Very quietly —
salt against the inside of the shaker.

Talk like glue.

The crackling of lips is in between.

The sound of bones is in your mouth.
They are washed like dishes and stacked in small piles.

Your tongue slides in the long rim of your lip.

Laughter clatters like a plate off the table.

Later, there is the sound of papers rolling.

You have been eating fish heads again.

Maybe you have been sucking oysters.

Maybe you have been telling someone stories,

or, maybe you have been walking juicily
on the fat grass of your memory.

And always by the time you have finished I am full.

Aunty Kare

When she sings
seagulls come out of her mouth.
I watch the shadow of one flying.

It folds neatly into the curtain.
It bumps a closed window.

The eyes of a photograph blink.

It bends around corners
and the wrinkles in faces.

It climbs on the shoulder of
the man asleep on the chair by the door.

It slips outside.
The dog walking past howls.

I watch the shadow of her voice
against the dull green ache of bush.

I watch it move in the air of an open cage.

I watch it fly along the straight edge of the beach.

I watch it press against the mouths of waves like a kiss.

I watch it circle back above us once
                              and then fly on without stopping.

Uncle Tu

If you want to see him go to a river.
Look under the round water.
Find the rock carved bluntly.
It should be greenstone.

Its eyes may swim to the surface like fish.

He is like that.

If you want to see him go to the top of a mountain.
Look down through the clouds.
Find the ground's face.
The eyes made of water. The volcanic nose.
His bush lips and unshaven stubble.
Find the deep lines that a stream makes —
the skull of rock at his temples blown smooth
by wind and rain and the falling of trees.

The immediate distance.

He is like that.

If you want to see him, go to a church.
The walls should be made of wood.
The pews will be oak.
Stand inside on the smooth floor.
Breathe in the smell of the polish.
Wait for the bell to be rung.

Listen to the strong sound of the hammer on the iron.
It should be clear.

He is like that.

If you want to see him go to a place where treasure is kept.
Stand over a glass box.
Look inside for things that are worn.
The blunt tiki.
The smooth handle on a walking stick.
The old korowai sleeping
with a head tucked beneath her feathers.

Find the stone mere chipped around the edges.

And he is like that.

Photo: Helen Wadsworth

Aunty Rongo

The things around you move.

Carpet scratches.

A table shifts its weight from leg to leg.
Windows open themselves in the morning to breathe.

Moonlight folds her blanket
and brushes the steps as she leaves.
The grass is wet with daisies.

A chair opens outward from the table.

The curved fridge by the window burps.
A teacup opens its mouth.
Crockery in the cabinet taps on the glass to be fed.
A knife stretches out beside its saucer.

The tablecloth measures the length of her skirt in the mirror.

Walls yawn.
They make gaps where they usually touch.

In the next room pillows argue on the couch.

Photographs on your wall wake up.
The chest of the TV heaves with sleep. The clock winds.
The mad chimes in the corner rock in the wind.

Yesterday's talk settles on the paint.
The long iron key in the lock stares.
The roof tightens in the sun.

When the sky is alone he sits at your back door and listens.
It is a full enough universe.

You are all that is left unsaid.

Aunty Maude

My eyes are paintbrushes.
They dip in the light that falls through your window.
They colour on the edge of your hair.

My eyes are crayons.
They draw wide lines around your face.
It will not stay inside them.

My eyes are pens.
They write that you move with the softness
of a white cloud on a blue day.

My eyes are chisels.
They carve you holding up the roof of a house.
Your breath is tukutuku.

My eyes are shutters.
They draw black lines in the footprints of a bird
that was drinking from the corner of your eye.

White is the snow on the peaks of your face.

My eyes are grapes.
Your smile plucks them from my empty
plate and swallows them.

Aunty Huia

I return from her house with the idea of her fingers. They are thin and black — the roots of pohutukawa. I am careful where I carry them in case they pinch.

I return from her house with the sound of her voice. There are sharp words left on the end of her sentences. Two I prise from my skin where they have stuck.

I return from her house with the smell of flax. It presses in an old book. When I open it again the leaves smell sweet as well as stale. For a moment I look around.

I return from her house with a piece of sky — that cloud which sits like a curled-up dog above her roof. The sound of barking comes from inside as I run.

I return from her house with the shape of her face. I carry it outstretched along the grass as though it is a pot of boiling water. At home I find a picture in a book of a roman emperor.

I return from her house with the taste of bread. My mouth walks round inside itself the way that people look at art inside a gallery. Butter runs against my tongue like wet paint.

I return from her house with the impression of her feet. They are as practical as hands. Her footsteps prepare the ground for walking as if they were plaiting long hair.

I return from her house with a piece of flax — to loop between the parts of her which I have left and carry them like car-keys in my hand — the way she carries a catch of snapper back home, at night, along the beach.

Aunty Flu does not live in Te Tii. She is from Whangape. She had been living in Parapara for over forty years when I met her.

Aunty Flu

"Kia ora."
"Tena koe pakeha."

There is no conversation in the next line.
There is a kiss.

"How are you?"
"I am well."
"Where have you been?"
"I have been working."
"Which way did you come?"
"I came the long way."
"I was looking but did not see you."

"What have you been doing?"

"I have been to the doctor. He is a pakeha doctor.
He said that I smoke too much.

I said 'Well doctor it is like this,
if I walk out of here I'm still going to smoke — you're not
paying for my smokes.' He said 'Are you taking your pills?'
I said I hadn't taken them for a week and I'm not dead yet.'

He said 'O — Mrs. Rewiti.'

Well I did, I said that. It is not his fault.
He is a good doctor. I took him a kete.

You look too skinny. Do you want a cup of tea?"

"I would."

"The kettle is over there."

"Kia ora."

"Tena koe pakeha."

There is no conversation in the next line.
There is a kiss.

"What have you been up to?"

"No, I have been well. I stopped smoking, just stopped.

They said to me 'Sorry aunty we should smoke outside'.
I said 'No it doesn't worry me. Smoke inside.
I don't want your bloomin smokes. Here have these.'
I gave them my smokes and that was it — well I never.

My mate said 'You should get some company.'
I said 'I already got company.'
I said 'I got three good mates here.' She said 'Who's that?'
I said 'The ones that don't back answer.'
That's Utu, Tipsy and Harley. They are my dogs, eh!

She said 'You need a man.' I said 'You get one yourself.'

Anyway you're getting fat. Do you want a cup of tea?"

"Yes, I'll get it."

"No, leave it alone. Just sit there."

I did.

I thought

"O — Mrs Rewiti."

WHAKAPAPA

i. the taniwha

My great great great great
grandfather was a taniwha.

He lived in the sky on the other side of the world.

His head rested between mountains.

His bed was made on a long white cloud.

His eyes were sunrise and sunset.

In his chest was the leaping of a fish.

His shoulders were a flock of birds rising off a beach,
the bend of wind inside their wings,
the balance of their feet like sticks.

His belly was a steaming loaf of bread at
the centre of a table full of people eating.

His legs were made from dark rock.
They showed through the grass of hills.

His toes were the crawling of animals in the soil,
the scatter of mice, the burning colours
on the back of beetles.

In his mouth was a great wind.

And when he tried to speak to us
with the roar of his voice we were scattered.

Sometimes through the steady
march of the sky I think he is looking for us.

His footsteps make the sound of thunder.

The changing shapes of cloud are his face.

His beard is the brushing of black rain.

His breath searches in the tops of trees
and shivers along the backs of my arms.

ii. the underworld

My great great great grandfather blew
across the sky and fell inside the open
mouth of war

                and this is all we know
that the ground covered up over the top
of him and that the grass grew back into
its place and that the sun smoothed over
the soil and that the clouds walked it flat
again.

        Silver water flows along the scar.

The creaking of earth at night is his voice.
His outline squeezes in the shape of hills.

iii. the tide

I have found shards of my great great
grandfather in the mouths of my old people.

Out of the sky he fell inside the sea and was swallowed.

He sailed on the fins of a dolphin.
He drank with sharks.
He watched the dancing of mermaids.

From serpents he was told the directions of the world,
the currents to take, the turns to be made at whirlpools.

He passed between great reefs.
He walked through forests of coral.
He clung underneath the belly of a whale.

One day he came to the other side of the world.

He found a place he did not know was there.

When he thought that it was firm he stood,
but his feet began to melt.

His arms became pools of water.
His belly rippled into circles.
His hair turned to white foam.

His eyes sat like paua on the bottom of the ocean.

He turned into the shape of the tide
that sweeps the shore like a stiff broom.

And there he has stayed never leaving and never quite arriving.

Sometimes on the edge of the sand
you will see him stand up to look for us.

His hands run into the cracks between rocks.

Sometimes you will see the moon
drag him from the beach by his ankles.

From there he will sink into the green sea.

He will make bubbles in the holes of crabs.
He will leave lines of seaweed on the sand.

iv. carrying baggage

My great great grandmother was a settler. She brought with her a magic suitcase. Out of it has come treasure, like old photographs of moustaches and petticoats, and like watches on chains kept in pockets, like pipes, and tables and chairs and china, like iron tools and iron beds and iron looks, like family bibles, like lace and embroidery, like shops, and selling flour and shoes and corn and hats, like sacks, like running writing and stamps, and letters for far away, like streets, like corners to put between them, like cars to put on them, like buildings to hold them down when it blows, like wharves to unpack more unpacking, like churches and banks and schools, like st johns and st marys, like bicycles with baskets, like wars from here and places more here than here, like monuments, like anzac day, like crosscut saws, like laws and the people that make them, like animals, like farms and friesians and separators, like bugs, like fenceposts and flagpoles and goalposts, like old folks homes and orphans, like factories, and milking sheds, like new ways of going to heaven and new ways of not, like weatherboards, like polling and voting and houses of parliament, like guy fawkes, like bumble bees and bottles of milk and going to dentists, like lawnmowers, like TVs and radios and good golly miss molly, like I just spent six months in a leaky boat, like front gardens and vegetable gardens and garden sheds and garden gnomes, like cars on blocks in the front yard, like the east tamaki tavern, like goats on the side of the road, like the smell of compost and of mangere on a damp day, like hedges, like newspapers and the womens weekly and time, like the market and interest rates and the CPI and the AAA and the GDP, like the TAB, like percentages, like saving for a rainy day, like bennie day, like south african referees, like royal tours and rugby tours and touring bands and western springs, like I'm absolutely buggered, like I knocked the bugger off, like I'm buggered if I know, like australians, like home-made ginger beer, like peanut slabs and mcdonalds and KFC and georgie pie, like the easter show, like flowers and shells and leis around tombstones, like necklaces around photographs, like the otara markets and taro and tapa and women in white hats going to church, like kumara chips and coke and L&P and hokey pokey, like flash houses in howick, like buckets and spades at christmas, like when are we going to be there, like bog and rusty cars, like fluffy dice, like make-up, like school C and UE and primer one and primer two, like the donkeys egg and miss pennyweather, like polytech, like knitting needles, like sticking plasters in the swimming pool, like wooden houses and brick houses and washhouses and state houses and mirror glass, like village six and village seven and the empire strikes back, like baseball caps, like the chicago bulls and number 23 and $250.00 sandshoes, like jaffas, like shopping centres and food courts and farmers cards and friday nights and foto island, and like whatever is still coming, and like whatever is still being unwrapped, and unveiled, and untied, and unspoken, and undone, and untidied, and unsaid, and unfolded, and unkempt, and untold, and unwritten, and unsolved, and unmet, and unleashed, and unravelled, and unpacked, and compacked, and impacked, and unpacked, and unpacked, and unpacked, and unpacked.

v. a pakeha spiritual

The father of the father of my father
was afraid that the sea would wash him away.
He cut the land into squares with his knife.
He lashed the soil onto his back.

He dug in the soft flesh of the earth.

The father of the father of my father
made the sound inside my chest of heartbeats.
They were his feet walking up the sides of a mountain.
They were his measured breaths in thin air.

He walked on the bent back of the land.

The father of the father of my father
carried summits under his arms through the clouds.
He made the earth into a mountain
He made it reach all the way up to God.

The sun made a ladder in the sky.

The father of the father of my father
built a church on the top of the world.
It had a window the shape of hands praying.
He sang hymns that drowned out the sea.

He hid in the hem of God's robe.

The father of the father of my father
is petrified now on a long ridge of granite.
An avalanche slips through his fingers.
The snow is turning his hair white.

He wears the wrinkles of rock.

The father of the father of my father
has a back the shape of a great mountain.
He is the same size now as his fear.
When I look at him I shade my eyes.

vi. the bird

My grandfather was a bird.

Underneath his white hair
he wore crayon-coloured feathers.

They were of boiling gold
and of burning red
and of drowning blue

One was green the colour of a single blade of grass.

When he walked ahead of me
I could see from his stride how he flew
in the branches of trees.

When his hand curled in my hair
I could feel him perching around me.

When he worked on the end of a shovel
I found how his arms spread wide in a turn.

And when he stood over a bed full of flowers
I saw that his eyes gathered what shone
on the ground for his nest.

When he was gone I remember him sitting in a tree
in a garden which he had planted.

And all the cries of morning were around him.

vii. the half moon

Chapter one
When he was born my father was cut in half. No one knew how it happened. For a long time we did not notice.

Chapter two
The half of my father which was left grew up strong enough for both of him. When he was a boy he wrestled a great bull to the ground. He took its most powerful leg and tied it to his hips.

Chapter three
When he was a youth my father threw himself against the green muscle of the land. He broke the mightiest branch from a great tree and sewed it to his shoulders for an arm.

Chapter four
When he was a man my father dug in the ground. He took the twisting tails of rivers and turned them where he chose. He brushed the hills from the soil as if he was clearing the table of food.

Chapter five
One day my father reached inside the sky to pluck the moon for his lost eye. From the gap which it left a half moon rose. My father's leg pawed in the dirt. His arm swayed like a tree in a storm.

Chapter six
While he slept that night the moon opened my father's skin and rained inside him. The world shook back and forth. The sea spilled. Where my father fought, the land creased like blankets into mountains. The inside of his muscles began to rust.

Chapter seven
When he became cold my father chopped away his arm for firewood. When he grew hungry he tore at his leg for food. One day he fell over onto his side. He looked like an old ship sinking in the sea.

Chapter eight
When my father stopped struggling the moon found a place beside him and lay down. He sewed a stitch of lightning between them. Fire burnt in their muscles. A curl of steam rose above them.

Chapter nine
When the steam cleared my father stood up. The world seemed a long way away. He stumbled to the edge of a lake to drink. When my father opened his eye a sprinkle of light began to spread across the water.

viii. a story

I would like to be a story.

Maybe my stomach could be the first notes of an opera.
It is soft and round. It could be sung by fat men
in black suits at the top of their voices.
It should wobble and bounce and echo.

Maybe my bones could be the rattle of dancing.
If they were hung in a doorway by the beach, they
would chime in the wind. Fingers could strum
the lines at the corners of my eyes when I smile.

Maybe my skin could be the pale screen of a movie.
Light catches through a window and draws pictures on me.
Cowboys roam the sun-drenched prairies on the back
of my arms. Gangsters move quietly in the shadows.

Maybe my hands could be the covers of a book.
They are bent over at the edges and well-thumbed.
People read carefully between the lines. They could
make stories from whatever they held between them.

Maybe my mouth could be a poem. It is so full of words.
I should take it down to a choppy sea and leave it on
the beach for the water to bubble on my tongue.

One day my ears could become shells.

My throat would make the sound of gulls.

Birds might pluck at my teeth for mussels.

My jaw would be driftwood.

And in time all that would be left is a simple conversation
Where the words are eroded to notes.

ix. pakeha dreaming

They have been drawing us again in the dirt

The gods

With a pale finger of light
from the bent knuckle of the moon

With a bone
from the stiff upper lips of my old people.

The shape of us is sharp:
The angle of the bones under our skin
The points on the corners of our property
The crunching grey metal road in our voices.

The shape of us is straight:
Down the edge of our noses
and along the soles of our feet.
Our teeth are almost at right angles.

The shape of us is measured:
Five shirts hung ironed in the wardrobe
My mother's running writing
Her freshly weeded garden.

The colour of us is light:

The creamy moon
        The inside of clouds
                The flesh of apples.

The shape of us is not quite neat:

An old radio with a wire stretched up the wall

The first page missing from a book

A watercolour with the paint still drying

Still waiting to see how our limbs work:

The stumbling in the walk of a foal
The yawning in the steps of children.

LEARNING
HOW TO HONGI

Te huihuinga ki waho

I have come from
so many places to meet here,

sliding crooked down one
hundred years of window pane

to collect like a drop of rain
on this wooden sill.

I am a small boy stealing apples.
My eyes peep over your fence.

It is a loose cover on an old book.

It is a crack of light through an open door.

It is a too-tight belt around a laughing belly.

Looking through this thin line
I wait as new to me as I am to you

while my feet sip the stone road
like a too-hot cup of tea.

Wero

That leaf
falling
is a taiaha

twisting

sharply

between light
and dark

with two lips

asking

WHAT are you doing here?

what ARE you doing here?

what are YOU doing here?

what are you DOING here?

what are you doing HERE?

and
as I
bend
down
to lift it
I wonder
what
I might
knock
over
trying
to pick
it up.

Karanga

Hey.
You.
There.
You.
With your eyes open
during prayer.

Come here.
Come on.
Come softly.

Pick up
these words
which the wind
blows through
howling
and weave.

Yes.
Stitch.
Like this.
And twist.
I'll twist
a basket
from the rope
from this rope
dragging,
being dragged,
from you.
It may hold
some riwai,
a blanket,
an embrace.
Perhaps it will hold

Weave.
What?

A word
into a word.

It is a knot.

Stitch.
Stitch.
I stitch
the ends.
Over, under.
Over, under.

It is a rope
pulling me to you.

It pulls me
to your calling voice.

It pulls me
to your shaking voice.

Is this the way?

your many dead
who squirm in the kete
like fish in the net.
Pulled in.
Woven in.
Bubbling.

Climb up.
Move up.
Stand up.
Here.

On the other side
of this page.

Under this cloak
we have made
from the scraps of
chewed up distance
between us —

A korowai
carried by its feathers
into the sky.

Stand here.
Stop here.
Wait here.

In the still.
In the biting still.
In the rising still.

In the still that curls
like a springing fern
over the closing distance
between us.

It is a mat.
It is too full
for sides
to hold.
It splits.

It is like
the pattern
on your skin.

Every line
is a loss.

Every line
is a joy.

It is carpet.
It is a path.
It is soft grass.

My feet
are cooled.

Haka

I want to know!
Don't I belong here?

I was born at Papa-kura.
My whenua turned the soil red.

My mother cried like a seagull.

Her ancestors are buried in Papa-toetoe.
Their old heads are white plumes.

My father held me to this
upside-down sky and I sneezed.

Am I not maori?

I want to know!
Do you belong here?

Where is Kupe from?
His canoe was a strange tree.

Could he feel what my people felt?

This place to rest from the sea.
This longing for home.

Where do the dead return to?
Hawaiki nui. Hawaiki roa. Hawaiki pamaomao.

Are you not pakeha?

Whakaekea

I leave my shoes by an empty peach tin.

It is used as an ashtray.

I leave my legs still standing inside them.

I leave my stomach in a pot in the kitchen.

My mouth hangs on a tree like a fish drying.

My ears listen for gossip.

My eyes roll down to the sea.

I stick my nose under a bench like chewing gum.

I leave my arms for the dog to play with.

What is left I take inside.

It is much later,
               after leaving,
                         that I find

I am wearing someone else's body again.

Karakia

for Hemi Epiha

Our Hemi,
who is on earth,
it was holy your prayer.
I fought with God over it
who wanted to take back to heaven
what he had heard on earth.
I said leave us our doubt
our failing doubt,
and forgive it our trespasses,
as we forgive ourselves
who trespass against us.
And lead us not into salvation
delivered of people;
for ours is a clasped hand
over the cower and the glory
and the never and ever
of man.

Mihi

What is a pakeha mihi?

I am from a photograph in a book
I found in the library.

I am from an old story my
aunty repaired before she died.

I am from a concrete land.
The stretching tile lids are my mountain.
The snaked black tar is my river.

I am from the deep green sea.
Her pounamu is around my neck.

I am a cross made from a thousand
mongreled hurts and loves and ordinary lives,

a suitcase full of people tucked beneath
my bed, sprung open.

I am a green log that has waited
five generations to smoulder,
I grasp the springing flame
and drive it into my chest.

I am from a city of lovers,
where the grass is sown on fire,

And so to my whare
of egg-shell tin.
Stand.

And to the soft
brown-bellied earth.
Rest.

And to the dead
worn silky around me.
Cling.

And to the dead who meet
bubbling like a wave into sand.
Sizzle.

And to the living
blown cackling like grass.
Rustle.

And to the living who meet
sipping each other like tea.
Drink.

And to this breath
all breathed before.
Be breathed again.

Waiata

At that place I call the-bend-in-the-road
I heard the sound of people singing.
Their voices were like smoke rising out of houses.
The wind whistled softly through his teeth.
I found verses everywhere.

At that place I call sitting-cross-legged-on-a-chair
you watched me clear a place to stay.
We coloured in the conversation with crayons.
I talked about the names of dogs.
When you asked me why I had come it was
the sound of knuckles knocking on a door.

At that place I call a-belly-full-of-people
I went to sleep on the sound of snoring.
The night rose like a tide to cover us.
In the morning you said ghosts had come
and poked me with a stick.
They said that I was fat enough to stay.
All I heard was crunching on the path outside.

At that place I call the-room-in-which-we-spoke
I ate a feast.
The walls held us like two pips inside an apple.
I listened to your voice when we were full.
It was the sound of tea pouring.

At that place I call the-cave-in-which-I-slept
I heard the rain play wild drums on my roof.
The night wore a short black dress.
Fire danced slowly with bare shoulders on the ceiling.
Water tapped a finger on a bucket through the night.

At that place I call taking-the-words-out-of-my-mouth
I heard my voice begin to sing.
The sun did not notice, the moon rolled over on its side.
The breeze continued, the birds were not disturbed.

My lips were pounding drums.
My feet were heathen dancing around a flame.

Koha

Aunty Kare gave me her recipe for making steamed-pudding.
She sits with me in church.

Carol showed me how to cook fried bread.

I put sausages in my boil ups.

Tom Kelly growled me for throwing fish heads to a dog.
Buck showed me how to tie a swivel.
Andy says "Big bait, big fish."

Aunty Rongo taught me how to speak maori.
Then she taught me poker.
She hides lotto tickets in her bible.

Aunty Riwa showed me how to play housie.

Uncle Bill made me eat kina.
And rotten corn.

He taught me to stand up and greet people.
And then to farewell them when they leave.

He told me stories of when he was a boy.

Twice Uncle Tu gave me his tokotoko.

Aunty Maude has been looking for a wife for me.

I stay in a tin shed by the beach.
It belongs to 'The Hood.'

Maybelline swears in the doorway. She is five.

I think I have been colonised.

Hongi

It has taken a long time
for this window
that I press against
to turn into
your soft nose.
Through this
I see more clearly,
in the misted breath,
what lies
on the other side
of my resting eyes.

Of my resting eyes
on the other side,
what lies
in the misted breath
I see more clearly
through this
your soft nose
turned into
that I press against.
For this window
it has taken a long time.

Whakanoa

This page is a pot.

It is well used.

It is dented.

I fill it with words
left at the bottom of their sacks.

They are soft like rubber.

Sprouting.

I fill it with bits of things
left half-spoken

those things left in a room
when everything else
is packed.

There are thoughts
without the fat trimmed off

There is thinking I started
and never finished.

There are bits of loving leftover,

boiling up.

The paper bubbles.

An old woman kneading bread.

Make a lot of noise
when you eat it.

Lick the plate until it is clean.

Sleep loudly in a chair
when you finish.

Let the light glisten
in the curve of your mouth.

Glossary

Hangi	earth oven
Hawaiki	*Hawaiki nui, Hawaiki roa, Hawaiki pamaomao* — traditional homeland of Maori people
Kahawai	a type of fish
Kete	flax bag
Kia ora	be well, a greeting or affirmation
Kina	sea urchin
Korowai	cloak
Kowhaiwhai	painted designs on the rafters of a meeting house
Kumara	sweet potato
Kupe	Polynesian discoverer of Aotearoa New Zealand
Lavalava	wrap-around cloth sometimes worn by Polynesian people
Marae	meeting place; often the focal point of a Maori community, a place to meet and discuss issues with facilities for eating, playing and sleeping
Mere	a short, flat weapon
Pakeha	a New Zealander of European descent
Palagi	Samoan term for a person of European descent
Paua	a shellfish, abalone
Pipi	a shellfish
Ponga	a native fern
Pounamu	greenstone
Poupou	a carved pillar in a meeting house, usually representing a person important to the tribe
Riwai	potato
Taiaha	a long staff for fighting
Taniwha	a monster, protective or malevolent
Tena koe	a greeting
Tiki	a popular motif in Maori carving — representing a person
Tokotoko	walking stick
Tui	a bird
Tukutuku	a criss-cross design used to decorate and to tell a story
Umu	Samoan earth oven
Whakapapa	genealogy
Whare	house, dwelling
Whenua	placenta, land

The following words from the sequence *Learning how to hongi* represent stages in a powhiri. This is the ceremony welcoming guests onto a marae via which they are accepted as part of the local community.

Te huihuinga ki waho	the gathering of people outside a marae, ie before they are called on
Wero	challenge
Karanga	call
Haka	posture dance
Whakaekea	the act of going onto the marae itself or into the meeting house
Karakia	prayer or blessing
Mihi	speech of greeting or acknowledgement
Waiata	song
Koha	gift
Hongi	pressing of noses between people; an exchange of breath
Whakanoa	literally to make common (non-sacred), used in the welcoming ceremony as the point where the hosts and guests eat together

OTHER POETRY BY GLENN COLQUHOUN

An Explanation of Poetry to My Father   2001
Playing God   2002

PUBLISHED BY STEELE ROBERTS